Alto Saxophone

Alfred's INSTRUMENTAL PLAY-ALONG

mp3 CD

Ultimate Movie
Instrumental Solos

Arranged by Bill Galliford, Ethan Neuburg, and Tod Edmondson
Recordings produced by Dan Warner, Doug Emery, Lee Levin and Artemis Music Limited.

© 2012 Alfred Music Publishing Co., Inc.
All Rights Reserved. Printed in USA.

ISBN-10: 0-7390-9189-1
ISBN-13: 978-0-7390-9189-0

Alfred

CONTENTS

AUGIE'S GREAT MUNICIPAL BAND

(from *Star Wars Episode I: The Phantom Menace*)

Music by
JOHN WILLIAMS

Track 2: Demo
Track 3: Play-Along

ACROSS THE STARS

(Love Theme from *Star Wars Episode II: Attack of the Clones*)

Track 4: Demo
Track 5: Play-Along

Music by
JOHN WILLIAMS

Across the Stars - 2 - 1

43 Appassionato

52

60

64

poco rit.

a tempo

rit. e dim.

ANAKIN'S THEME

(from *Star Wars Episode I: The Phantom Menace*)

Track 6: Demo
Track 7: Play-Along

Music by
JOHN WILLIAMS

Anakin's Theme - 2 - 1

BATTLE OF THE HEROES

(from *Star Wars Episode III: Revenge of the Sith*)

Music by
JOHN WILLIAMS

Battle of the Heroes - 2 - 1

CAN YOU READ MY MIND?

(Love Theme from *Superman*)

Words by LESLIE BRICUSSE
Music by JOHN WILLIAMS

Track 10: Demo
Track 11: Play-Along

CONCERNING HOBBITS

(from *The Lord of the Rings: The Fellowship of the Ring*)

Track 12: Demo
Track 13: Play-Along

Music by
HOWARD SHORE

CANTINA BAND
(from *Star Wars Episode IV: A New Hope*)

Music by
JOHN WILLIAMS

Track 14: Demo
Track 15: Play-Along

Moderately fast ragtime ($\bf d$ = 112)

To Coda ⊕

Cantina Band - 2 - 1

DIAMONDS ARE FOREVER

Track 16: Demo
Track 17: Play-Along

Music by JOHN BARRY
Lyric by DON BLACK

Moderately (♩ = 104)

DOUBLE TROUBLE
(from *Harry Potter and the Prisoner of Azkaban*)

Music by
JOHN WILLIAMS

DING-DONG! THE WITCH IS DEAD

(from *The Wizard of Oz*)

Track 20: Demo
Track 21: Play-Along

Music by HAROLD ARLEN
Lyric by E.Y. HARBURG

Ding-Dong! The Witch Is Dead - 2 - 1

DUEL OF THE FATES
(from *Star Wars Episode I: The Phantom Menace*)

Track 22: Demo
Track 23: Play-Along

Music by
JOHN WILLIAMS

Duel of the Fates - 2 - 1

EVENSTAR

(from *The Lord of the Rings: The Two Towers*)

Music by HOWARD SHORE
Text by J.R.R. TOLKIEN

FOLLOW THE YELLOW BRICK ROAD/ WE'RE OFF TO SEE THE WIZARD

(from *The Wizard of Oz*)

Track 26: Demo
Track 27: Play-Along

Music by HAROLD ARLEN
Lyric by E.Y. HARBURG

FAMILY PORTRAIT

(from *Harry Potter and the Sorcerer's Stone*)

Track 28: Demo
Track 29: Play-Along

Music by
JOHN WILLIAMS

Slowly, with expression (♩ = 80)

* An easier 8th note alternative figure has been provided.

Family Portrait - 2 - 1

*B♯ = C♮
**E♯ = F♮

FAWKES THE PHOENIX
(from *Harry Potter and the Chamber of Secrets*)

Music by
JOHN WILLIAMS

Fawkes the Phoenix - 2 - 1

*An easier 8th-note alternative figure has been provided.

FOR YOUR EYES ONLY

Track 32: Demo
Track 33: Play-Along

Music by BILL CONTI
Lyrics by MICHAEL LEESON

FROM RUSSIA WITH LOVE

Track 34: Demo
Track 35: Play-Along

Words and Music by
LIONEL BART

GOLDFINGER

Track 36: Demo
Track 37: Play-Along

Music by JOHN BARRY
Lyrics by LESLIE BRICUSSE
and ANTHONY NEWLEY

HARRY'S WONDROUS WORLD

(from *Harry Potter and the Sorcerer's Stone*)

Track 38: Demo
Track 39: Play-Along

Music by
JOHN WILLIAMS

Harry's Wondrous World - 3 - 1

*A# = B♭

Stately and nobly

legato

101

117

a tempo

rit.

GOLLUM'S SONG

(from *The Lord of the Rings: The Two Towers*)

Track 40: Demo
Track 41: Play-Along

Music by HOWARD SHORE
Words by FRAN WALSH

Moderately, flowing (♩ = 104)

Gollum's Song - 2 - 1

Gollum's Song - 2 - 2

GONNA FLY NOW
(Theme from *Rocky*)

Track 42: Demo
Track 43: Play-Along

Words and Music by
BILL CONTI, AYN ROBBINS
and CAROL CONNORS

Moderately ♩ = 96

Gonna Fly Now - 2 - 1

Track 44: Demo
Track 45: Play-Along

HEDWIG'S THEME

(from *Harry Potter and the Sorcerer's Stone*)

Music by
JOHN WILLIAMS

I SWEAR

(from *The Social Network*)

Words and Music by
GARY BAKER and FRANK MYERS

IF I ONLY HAD A BRAIN
(from *The Wizard of Oz*)

Track 48: Demo
Track 49: Play-Along

Music by HAROLD ARLEN
Lyric by E.Y. HARBURG

IN DREAMS

(from *The Lord of the Rings: The Fellowship of the Ring*)

Track 50: Demo
Track 51: Play-Along

Words and Music by
FRAN WALSH and
HOWARD SHORE

Moderately slow (♩ = 76)

JAMES BOND THEME

(from *Dr. No*)

By
MONTY NORMAN

Track 52: Demo
Track 53: Play-Along

Moderately bright (♩ = 138)

LEAVING HOGWARTS
(from *Harry Potter and the Sorcerer's Stone*)

Music by
JOHN WILLIAMS

Track 56: Demo
Track 57: Play-Along

LILY'S THEME

(Main Theme from *Harry Potter and the Deathly Hallows, Part 2*)

Slowly, with expression (♩ = 72)

Music by
ALEXANDRE DESPLAT

MANY MEETINGS

(from *The Lord of the Rings: The Fellowship of the Ring*)

Track 58: Demo
Track 59: Play-Along

Music by
HOWARD SHORE

LIVE AND LET DIE

Words and Music by
PAUL McCARTNEY and
LINDA McCARTNEY

Track 60: Demo
Track 61: Play-Along

Live and Let Die - 2 - 1

MARION'S THEME

(from *Raiders of the Lost Ark*)

Music by
JOHN WILLIAMS

Track 62: Demo
Track 63: Play-Along

MAY THE FORCE BE WITH YOU

(from *Star Wars Episode IV: A New Hope*)

Music by
JOHN WILLIAMS

Track 64: Demo
Track 65: Play-Along

NOBODY DOES IT BETTER

(from *The Spy Who Loved Me*)

Track 66: Demo
Track 67: Play-Along

Music by MARVIN HAMLISCH
Lyrics by CAROLE BAYER SAGER

OBLIVIATE
(from *Harry Potter and the Deathly Hallows, Part 2*)

Track 68: Demo
Track 69: Play-Along

Music by
ALEXANDRE DESPLAT

Track 70: Demo
Track 71: Play-Along

ON HER MAJESTY'S
SECRET SERVICE

By JOHN BARRY

Maestoso (♩ = 120)

Track 72: Demo
Track 73: Play-Along

(YOU'RE OUT OF THE WOODS)

OPTIMISTIC VOICES

(from *The Wizard of Oz*)

Lyric by
E.Y. HARBURG

Music by
HAROLD ARLEN and
HERBERT STOTHART

Moderately bright ($\quad$ = 104)

Track 74: Demo
Track 75: Play-Along

OVER THE RAINBOW

(from *The Wizard of Oz*)

Lyric by
E.Y. HARBURG

Music by
HAROLD ARLEN

Slowly, with expression ($\quarternote = 88$)

PRINCESS LEIA'S THEME

(from *Star Wars Episode IV: A New Hope*)

Music by
JOHN WILLIAMS

RAIDERS MARCH

(from *Raiders of the Lost Ark*)

Music by
JOHN WILLIAMS

Track 78: Demo
Track 79: Play-Along

March (♩ = 126)

Raiders March - 2 - 1

Track 80: Demo
Track 81: Play-Along

ROHAN
(from *The Lord of the Rings: The Two Towers*)

Text by
J.R.R. TOLKIEN

Music by
HOWARD SHORE

Moderately (♩ = 76)
(Tempo click)

SONG FROM M*A*S*H
(Suicide Is Painless)

Track 82: Demo
Track 83: Play-Along

Words and Music by
MIKE ALTMAN and JOHNNY MANDEL

STAR WARS
(Main Theme)
(from *Star Wars Episode IV: A New Hope*)

Music by
JOHN WILLIAMS

Track 84: Demo
Track 85: Play-Along

STATUES
(from *Harry Potter and the Deathly Hallows, Part 2*)

By
ALEXANDRE DESPLAT

Track 86: Demo
Track 87: Play-Along

Moderately, with movement (♩ = 132)

THE STEWARD OF GONDOR

(from *The Lord of the Rings: The Return of the King*)

Track 88: Demo
Track 89: Play-Along

Lyrics by
J.R.R. TOLKIEN
Adapted by
PHILIPPA BOYENS

Music by
HOWARD SHORE
Contains the Composition "The Edge Of Night"
Melody by **BILLY BOYD**

Track 90: Demo
Track 91: Play-Along

THE BLACK RIDER
(from *The Lord of the Rings: The Fellowship of the Ring*)

Music by
HOWARD SHORE

THEME FROM SUPERMAN

Track 92: Demo
Track 93: Play-Along

Music by
JOHN WILLIAMS

Theme from Superman - 2 - 1

Track 94: Demo
Track 95: Play-Along

THE ARENA
(from *Star Wars Episode II: Attack of the Clones*)

Music by
JOHN WILLIAMS

The Arena - 2 - 1

THE IMPERIAL MARCH
(DARTH VADER'S THEME)

(from *Star Wars Episode V: The Empire Strikes Back*)

Track 96: Demo
Track 97: Play-Along

Music by
JOHN WILLIAMS

THE LULLABY LEAGUE/
THE LOLLIPOP GUILD/
WE WELCOME YOU TO MUNCHKINLAND

(from *The Wizard of Oz*)

Track 98: Demo
Track 99: Play-Along

Music by HAROLD ARLEN
Lyric by E.Y. HARBURG

THE MEADOW PICNIC
(from *Star Wars Episode II: Attack of the Clones*)

Track 100: Demo
Track 101: Play-Along

Music by
JOHN WILLIAMS

THE MERRY OLD LAND OF OZ

(from *The Wizard of Oz*)

Track 102: Demo
Track 103: Play-Along

Music by HAROLD ARLEN
Lyric by E.Y. HARBURG

THE NOTEBOOK
(Main Title)

Track 104: Demo
Track 105: Play-Along

Written by
AARON ZIGMAN

THE PROPHECY

(from The Lord of the Rings: The Fellowship of the Ring)

Track 106: Demo
Track 107: Play-Along

Music by HOWARD SHORE
Text by J.R.R. TOLKIEN
Adapted by PHILLIPPA BOYENS

THE PINK PANTHER

(from *The Pink Panther*)

Track 108: Demo
Track 109: Play-Along

By HENRY MANCINI

The Pink Panther - 2 - 1

THE THRONE ROOM

(from *Star Wars Episode IV: A New Hope*)

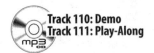

Track 110: Demo
Track 111: Play-Along

Music by
JOHN WILLIAMS

The Throne Room - 2 - 1

The Throne Room - 2 - 2

THUNDERBALL
(Main Theme)

Music by JOHN BARRY
Lyric by DON BLACK

Track 112: Demo
Track 113: Play-Along

TOMORROW NEVER DIES

Track 114: Demo
Track 115: Play-Along

Words and Music by
SHERYL CROW and
MITCHELL FROOM

WIZARD WHEEZES

(from *Harry Potter and the Half-Blood Prince*)

Track 116: Demo
Track 117: Play-Along

Music by
NICHOLAS HOOPER

Wizard Wheezes - 2 - 1

WONKA'S WELCOME SONG

(from *Charlie and the Chocolate Factory*)

Words by JOHN AUGUST and DANNY ELFMAN
Music by DANNY ELFMAN

(À la yodel)

YOU ONLY LIVE TWICE

Track 120: Demo
Track 121: Play-Along

Music by JOHN BARRY
Lyric by LESLIE BRICUSSE

PARTS OF AN ALTO SAXOPHONE AND FINGERING CHART

* When there are two fingerings given for a note, use the first one unless the alternate fingering is suggested.

* When two enharmonic notes are given together (F♯ and B♭ for example,) they sound the same pitch and are played the same way.

* Both pearl keys are pressed with the Left Hand 1st finger.

INSTRUMENTAL SOLOS

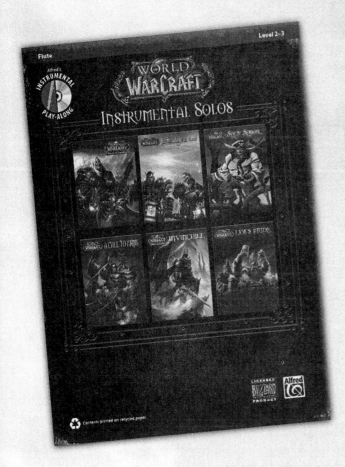

This instrumental series contains themes from Blizzard Entertainment's popular massively multiplayer online role-playing game and includes 4 pages of art from the World of Warcraft universe. The compatible arrangements are carefully edited for the Level 2–3 player, and include an accompaniment CD which features a demo track and play-along track. Titles: Lion's Pride • The Shaping of the World • Pig and Whistle • Slaughtered Lamb • Invincible • A Call to Arms • Gates of the Black Temple • Salty Sailor • Wrath of the Lich King • Garden of Life.

(00-36626) | Flute Book & CD | $12.99

(00-36629) | Clarinet Book & CD | $12.99

(00-36632) | Alto Sax Book & CD | $12.99

(00-36635) | Tenor Sax Book & CD | $12.99

(00-36638) | Trumpet Book & CD | $12.99

(00-36641) | Horn in F Book & CD | $12.99

(00-36644) | Trombone Book & CD | $12.99

(00-36647) | Piano Acc. Book & CD | $14.99

(00-36650) | Violin Book & CD | $16.99

(00-36653) | Viola Book & CD | $16.99

(00-36656) | Cello Book & CD | $16.99

Harry Potter

INSTRUMENTAL SOLOS

Play-along with the best-known themes from the Harry Potter film series! The compatible arrangements are carefully edited for the Level 2–3 player, and include an accompaniment CD which features a demo track and play-along track.

Titles: Double Trouble • Family Portrait • Farewell to Dobby • Fawkes the Phoenix • Fireworks • Harry in Winter • Harry's Wondrous World • Hedwig's Theme • Hogwarts' Hymn • Hogwarts' March • Leaving Hogwarts • Lily's Theme • Obliviate • Statues • A Window to the Past • Wizard Wheezes.

(00-39211) | Flute Book & CD | $12.99

(00-39214) | Clarinet Book & CD | $12.99

(00-39217) | Alto Sax Book & CD | $12.99

(00-39220) | Tenor Sax Book & CD | $12.99

(00-39223) | Trumpet Book & CD | $12.99

(00-39226) | Horn in F Book & CD | $12.99

(00-39229) | Trombone Book & CD | $12.99

(00-39232) | Piano Acc. Book & CD | $18.99

(00-39235) | Violin Book & CD | $18.99

(00-39238) | Viola Book & CD | $18.99

(00-39241) | Cello Book & CD | $18.99